Summary
of

Beartown
Fredrik Backman

Conversation Starters

By BookHabits

Tips for Using BookHabits Conversation Starters:

EVERY GOOD BOOK CONTAINS A WORLD FAR DEEPER THAN the surface of its pages. The characters and their world come alive through the words on the pages, yet the characters and its world still live on. Questions herein are designed to bring us beneath the surface of the page and invite us into the world that lives on. These questions can be used to:

- Foster a deeper understanding of the book
- Promote an atmosphere of discussion for groups
- Assist in the study of the book, either individually or corporately
- Explore unseen realms of the book as never seen before

About Us:

THROUGH YEARS OF EXPERIENCE AND FIELD EXPERTISE, from newspaper featured book clubs to local library chapters, *BookHabits* can bring your book discussion to life. Host your book party as we discuss some of today's most widely read books.

Table of Contents

Introducing *Beartown*

BEARTOWN IS THE LATEST OF SWEDISH WRITER FREDRIK BACKMAN'S novels that have gained the admiration of readers worldwide for his engaging storytelling style. Known for the bestselling debut novel *A Man Called Ove* which hit the New York Times bestseller list in 2015 and remaining there for 42 weeks, Backman has created a following since then with other equally highly-praised novels. *My Grandmother Asked Me To Tell You She's Sorry* followed *Ove*, and after that *Britt-Marie Was Here*. While the past three novels have protagonists who are quirky but endearing, *Beartown* is a departure from this signature Backman style. The author expands his depth and range as he tackles the dark issues involved in sports fanaticism gone overboard.

Beartown is a town threatened with extinction as its economy suffers stagnation and the forest slowly creeps in to reclaim abandoned houses left by former residents who leave town in search of better opportunities. The townspeople have one thing going for them though--ice hockey. Every boy in town is trained to play the game as early as possible. In the past, the town produced hockey players who went on to play for the NHL . Peter Andersson is one of them, but he is retired now due to an injury, and has returned to Beartown with his wife and two kids to become the general manager for the junior team. If Beartown is to rise from its stagnation, it is hockey that will do it and Peter will help make this happen. Kira, Peter's wife is a mother and a lawyer who chooses to work while being a mother to their children. She is not a typical mother, at least not to Beartown residents who are not used to seeing a mother who works outside the home. Maya, their 15-year-old daughter, does not share Peter's passion for sports; she prefers playing the guitar. She however understands her father when he starts talking about hockey.

The junior team has managed to reach the semifinals. Seventeen year-old Kevin is one of the finest players Beartown has ever seen. He leads the team that will bring honor to Beartown and along with it, economic opportunities that will revive the town. Much depends on Kevin and his teammates, particularly Benji who acts as Kevin's supporting player so the star player could perform his winning moves. On the night after a game, Kevin assaults Maya. The town is thrown into chaos as many rally around their hockey star.

Peter and his family find themselves besieged as they try to bring justice for Maya.

Backman divides the novel into the past and the present. The present shows the townspeople dealing with the repercussions of what happened in the past. The story has ten major characters whom Backman provides in-depth portrayal even as they tell their perspective of the events happening in Beartown. What results are layers and layers of stories from the different characters? Backman uses repetition of certain words and phrases to give new meanings every time and emphasizes the themes. Readers are thus made aware of the full implication of the repeated words and phrases.

The novel shows how sports can be a motivating factor that bring a community together, but is also a vehicle for negative beliefs such as racism, sexism, and politics. The young boys are taught by their leaders how to stay committed, disciplined and take responsibility, but outside the rink they act with a sense of entitlement, are exclusionary, and arrogant. The parents fail to teach them how to be kind and responsible adults outside the game. The novel touches on racism, with the character of Amat as the outsider who attracts racist attitudes from townspeople. Amat is the son of an immigrant woman. He is not strong or big but he is faster than anyone on ice, thus making him a valued hockey player. Another theme is of sexism and the violence that is condoned when sports players and their fans fail to be disciplined. Kevin's sense of entitlement when he raped Maya is a display of sexist attitudes adopted among sports players and their supporters. Related to this is the attitude of homophobia which runs among sexist men who feel threatened by other men of different gender preference. Backman likewise explored the issue of trauma among victims of violence and how this affects the entirety of one's life. Backman's focus on the community of Beartown shows how people are bonded together in their racist and exclusionary attitudes, and do not allow outsiders to affect their lives. The group thinking that prevails prevents people from acting for what is right.

Unlike his previous novels which focus on a central character, Backman focuses on the whole town to tell the story of Beartown. The *Washington Times* review says Backman showcases his "astonishing depth" in portraying the many characters in the novel, and his "broad range" as a writer. His ability to make readers understand the feelings of the many different characters in the novel is outstanding. And like his previous novels, *Beartown* has characters significant for their tenacity in picking up the pieces from a personal tragedy.

Discussion Questions

"Get Ready to Enter a New World"

Tip: Begin with questions dealing with broader issues to ensure ample time for quality discussions. Read through all discussion questions before engaging.

~~~

question 1

Beartown is at the edge of the forest. It is barely surviving and the forest
slowly reclaims the land where houses have been abandoned. What are the
factors leading to the slow demise of the town? Why is the town economy not
strong enough to sustain the people?

~~~

~~~

question 2

Beartown's remaining hope for revival is its youth hockey team. The
members of the team are teenagers who have to bear the weight of
expectations from their elders. Do you think it is fair for the adults to expect
much from the young boys? Is their hope for an economic revival for the
town a worthy reason for putting pressure on the boys?

~~~

question 3

The hockey club's leaders- David, Sune, and Peter- wanted to make sure that the young players win the youth tournament. The townspeople expect much from them. Apart from hockey training, do you think the boys are trained as well in handling the pressure they've been subjected to? Did their parents prepare them to handle the pressure?

~~~

question 4

Being members of a sports team teaches the young hockey players the values of responsibility, loyalty, and commitment, but it also encourages aggression, exclusivity and arrogance. Are the positive values useful in daily life? Do the players fail to curb their aggression and other negative traits when outside the game? In what instances?

~~~

~~~

question 5

Like boys their age, the hockey players enjoy having a good time and living for the moment instead of living up to the town's expectations of them as heroes. They are however forced to grow up quickly as they face adult realities. How has their experience influenced them later in their adult lives? How is Amat changed by his hockey experience? What about Bobo, Kevin and Benji?

~~~

~~~

question 6

Kira is a mother and a lawyer. Her work keeps her busy and does not allow
her to be the traditional mother, unlike most women in Beartown. Do you
think her job is important to her? Would you choose to be a working mother
like her, given the choice? Why?

~~~

~~~

question 7

Maya is an artistic and strong-willed girl. She is not crazy about hockey but understands her father who is passionate about it. How has the violence against her changed her as a person? How does her final act change her future?

~~~

~~~

question 8

Peter is passionate about hockey because it challenges him to give his best.
When Maya tells him and Kira about the assault done by the hockey boys, he
drops his coffee cup which shatters into pieces. What does his reaction to
Maya's revelation say about him as a father? Do you think he did his best to
find justice for Maya?

~~~

~~~

question 9

Backman uses repetition of certain words throughout the novel. In the first part of the book the words "bang bang bang" are repeated in between paragraphs. Why do you think the author repeats the same word over and over again? What is he trying to emphasize?

~~~

~~~

question 10

Backman breaks the novel into two parts-- the past and the present. In the present, the townspeople are still dealing with the consequences of what happened in the past. Do you think the town is forever changed because of the past? In what way? Can they recover from the past so that the future can be better?

~~~

question 11

Benji and Kevin are a team. Kevin plays good hockey because Benji plays
his part well. Benji also never lets his coach down. Off the ice, he helps keep
Kevin away from trouble. What does this say of Benji's character? Would
you want to have a friend like Benji?

~~~

~~~

question 12

Backman portrays how sports fans can put their love of sports above human
values of empathy, kindness, justice, and doing what is right. When Maya is
assaulted by the star player of the hockey team, the townspeople and sports
community express disapproval for Maya instead of punishing the perpetrator
of violence. Why do you think people can easily forget their values and
principles in defense of the sport? How do you feel about people who love
sports more than being right and fair?

~~~

~~~

question 13

The novel has ten different characters whose stories are told. This gives a general view of what is happening to the community of Beartown. Do you think the author was effective in portraying Beartown through the lives of the ten characters? Do you get an in-depth understanding of each of the characters despite the fact that there are ten of them?

~~~

~~~

question 14

Events are unfolded with each of the characters telling their perspective.
Different perspectives of Maya, Kevin, Peter and the different members of
the town create layer upon layer of stories. How does this affect the
storytelling process? How does it affect you as a reader? Do you feel like you
are going through a maze?

~~~

~~~

question 15

Amat is the son of an immigrant woman. He is not strong or big but he is faster than anyone on ice, thus making him a valued hockey player. How does Amat navigate racist attitudes of the people of Beartown? What values enable him to face racism?

~~~

~~~

question 16

Beartown is written by Swedish bestselling author of *A Man Called Ove*,
Fredrik Backman. His other novels before *Beartown* are similarly bestsellers
in Sweden. *Beartown* is different from his previous bestsellers because it
highlights a community instead of a single central protagonist which the other
novels are famous for. Do you think readers will love Backman's new book
despite its difference from other Backman novels? Why? Why not?

~~~

~~~

question 17

The *Washington Times* review says Backman's *Beartown* establishes his "astonishing depth" and his "broad range" as a writer. He also has the ability to make readers understand the feelings of the many different characters in the novel. Do you agree with the review? Can you cite an example of his "astonishing depth"?

~~~

~~~

question 18

Star2.com review compares *Beartown* to Backman's other novels - *A Man
Called Ove* and *Britt-Marie Was Here*. The review says all three novels have
characters that have the tenacity to pick up the pieces from a personal tragedy.
Who among the Beartown characters do you think is among the sturdiest?
Why?

~~~

~~~

question 19

StarTribune.com review thinks *Beartown* is a "universal story of homophobia, sexism and politics." The story could happen anywhere, not just in Sweden. Can you cite examples of places where the story of Beartown has happened? In what way are homophobia, sexism and politics practiced in these similar places?

~~~

~~~

question 20

USATODAY.com review says Backman's theme in the book is about how hockey players are regarded as "products more than people." How is this theme shown in the novel? Who are the people who regard the hockey players as products?

~~~

Introducing the Author

FREDERIK BACKMAN FIRST BECAME KNOWN FOR HIS DEBUT novel *A Man Called Ove* when it achieved the New York Times bestseller status in 2015. Producing two more bestselling novels in Sweden afterwards, Backman now has his fans eager for his latest work, *Beartown*. *Ove's* success came in slow and it took Backman many rejections from Swedish publishers before he could find one who believed in the novel's merits. It became an overnight success in Sweden in 2012. In 2014, it was published in the US and steadily reached the bestseller list after 18 months. His books are now being published in more than 25 languages.

Backman lives in Stockholm with his wife and two kids. He was a prolific blogger and a college drop-out who worked as a forklift driver before he published his first novel. He worked during evening and weekend shifts and spent the day hours writing his book. His readers love his novels for the quirky protagonists who end up becoming loveable as Backman worked to portray them in-depth. With *Beartown*, his readers are surprised by a change in theme and in the number of protagonists; this time, it is the whole community that he writes about. Backman says despite the difference in his new novel, it is still a story about human beings told in a way that he did with his previous novels. *Beartown*, however, is painted darker and more serious. He wanted to write about his love for sports and how important it is for him, adding in the dark aspects.

Backman grew up loving ice hockey, but it was the one sport he could not play as a child. He was fragile as a boy and always ended up injured every time he played it. There are things he finds dark about the sport despite his fascination with the game. While some young players do well under immense pressure, he knows that a lot of players also give in to the pressures from parents who expect them to perform well. In the novel, he shows how parents get mad and act as bullies on the sidelines as they watch their kids play.

Backman says he views writing as a hobby, not as a career choice. His father thinks his writing is probably something that he won't be doing for the rest of his life and Backman himself agrees. He can see himself going back to having a real job and he will be just as happy. He started writing his first novel as blog entries. People around him found his account of the man called

Ove very funny. It was taken from a real life incident which he later on developed upon the advice of his readers. About his novel *Britt-Marie Was Here*, he says its theme of fear of dying is crucial to all of his writing. *Britt-Marie* is considered a "low-intensity adventure", much like *Star Wars* and *Lord of the Rings.* It does not have sword fights and dragon fights, but it has the same basic theme-- the search for one's destiny. He admits he is better at telling stories than dealing with language. He rewrote *his* second novel 50 times but his third novel was rewritten five times. He claims he has no real formula for writing his stories.

Fireside Questions

"What would you do?"

Tip: These questions can be a fun exercise as it spurs creativity among the readers by allowing alternate scene endings and "if this was you" questions.

~~~

question 21

Fredrik Backman wrote Beartown as a way to express his love of sports and what it means to him. He also wanted to express the dark side of it. What is the dark side of sports that Backman highlighted in *Beartown?* In what way does he express his love of sports in the novel? Can you cite certain passages that show this?

~~~

~~~

question 22

Before publishing his first novel, Backman worked as a forklift driver at a food warehouse. He worked at nights and weekends so he can have the day time to write his novel. Do you think his choice of job supported his writing? Why?

~~~

~~~

question 23

Backman portrayed how young people are forced to carry the burden of their parents' expectations. The whole town looks to them to revive the economy and bring more jobs and income by winning the hockey championships. Do you think the author favors this kind of responsibility put on the young boys' shoulders? Why? Why not?

~~~

~~~

question 24

The author portrays how mob thinking can encourage athletes not to take
responsibility for a crime they are guilty of. In Beartown, parents and
supporters of the hockey team went against Peter and his family when Maya
filed charges against Kevin. Why do you think sports fans think athletes are
not responsible for wrongdoing? Why do you think they treat athletes as
demigods who can do no wrong?

~~~

~~~

question 25

The author was able to explain the game of hockey to readers who are not familiar with the game. He avoided technical jargon and made hockey appealing to those who don't care much about the game. Did you get a better understanding of hockey by reading the novel? Does it make you want to watch a live hockey game because of what you read?

~~~

~~~

question 26

Kevin is the golden boy of hockey and Beartown believes he will lead the team to victory and redemption for the town. When he is blamed for the assault against Maya, a lot of townspeople did not believe he is guilty. If you were Kevin's parents, would you have defended him even if you knew he was guilty? Why? Why not?

~~~

~~~

question 27

Maya is the artistic and strong-willed girl who eventually becomes the victim
of sexism in town. If she chose to keep quiet about the rape incident, how
would the story turned out? Would you have kept quiet if you were Maya?

~~~

~~~

question 28

Backman set the story in a small town in Sweden. If the story was set in the US, would it have the same themes of racism, sexism, and deification of athletes into demigods? Are these issues the same for America?

~~~

~~~

question 29

Ice hockey is the sport that everybody in Beartown is crazy about. Boys are taught how to play the game as early as they can. If the author used another sports like soccer or basketball instead, do you think sports fans would have the same attitudes around the sport? Would they still look at athletes as incapable of doing wrong? Would they defend the athletes right or wrong?

~~~

~~~

question 30

Beartown turned against Maya and her family when she implicated Kevin in her assault. If many of the townspeople decided to defend Maya, how would the story be different? How would it have ended?

~~~

Top 10 Amazing Facts

~~~

Top Fact #10

Backman's past novels focused on single characters on whom the story revolved. *Beartown* is different from his other novels because he focuses on a community instead of single protagonists. It shows Backman's evolving talent as a writer.

~~~

~~~

Top Fact #9

Backman admits he was a "very fragile kid". He tried to play hockey but he got hurt often. Despite this, he grew up following the Swedish Hockey League and the NHL. His interest in hockey is called by his wife a "serious mental issue."

~~~

~~~

Top Fact #8

The troubling aspects of hockey culture are portrayed in the novel, including overbearing parents who pressure their teen kids to perform well while watching on the sidelines. Backman's research on the subject included talking to former NHL players and their wives, current Swedish Elite players, parents and kids.

~~~

~~~

Top Fact #7

Sports sets up young people to become demigods if they're good players. But many of them cannot take the pressure and expectations. Backman comments on this through the novel by showing it is dangerous for teenagers to grow up with this notion.

~~~

~~~

Top Fact #6

For his research on trauma victims, Backman spoke to trauma survivors to understand its effects. He wanted to understand the shaming process carried out by the mob who defend famous athletes just because athletes are good at sports. The mob tries to destroy an accuser in many ways it can.

~~~

~~~

Top Fact #5

Beartown was originally written for a TV series. Backman got frustrated with the very slow process and was advised by his agent and wife that he should write it as a novel instead.

~~~

~~~

Top Fact #4

A minor character in the novel is Sune, Peter's coach since he was a young member of Beartown's A-team. The sponsors want him fired and suggest to Peter that he be the one to tell the old coach.

~~~

Top Fact #3

The novel is notable for its sly humor. An example is how the club president's table manners is described: as if he "actually misunderstood the whole concept of eating."

~~~

~~~

Top Fact #2

Backman is lauded for explaining ice hockey to readers without using technical jargon. His explanations make hockey details interesting and make readers appreciate the sport.

~~~

~~~

Top Fact #1

One of Backman's favorite books as a young boy was *Harry Potter: The Complete Series*. He says he still wishes he could be 7 years old again just to read the book for the first time. There are certain things in *Harry Potter* that adults can never fully understand, he says.

~~~

Quiz Questions

"Ready to Announce the Winners?"

Tip: Create a leaderboard and track scores to see who gets the most correct answers. Winners required. Prizes optional.

~~~

quiz question 1

Fredrik Backman first became known for his debut novel
_____. It hit the New York Times bestseller list in 2015 and
stayed there for 42 weeks.

~~~

~~~

quiz question 2

_____ used to be a star player in Beartown and went on to play for the NHL. He retired due to an injury and has taken over as the general manager of Beartown's junior hockey team.

~~~

~~~

quiz question 3

True or False: Kevin is one of the finest players Beartown has ever seen. Beartown depends on him and his teammates to revive the town's stagnant economy.

~~~

~~~

quiz question 4

True or False: Backman focuses the story of Beartown on just two central characters. The narrative is based on the perspective of these two characters.

~~~

~~~

quiz question 5

True or False: Backman uses repetition of certain words and phrases as a technique to tell the story. Repetition gives new meanings every time and emphasizes the theme. Readers are made aware of the full implication of the repeated words and phrases.

~~~

~~~

quiz question 6

_____ is the son of an immigrant woman. He is not strong or big but he is faster than anyone on ice, thus making him a valued hockey player.

~~~

quiz question 7

True or False: Like boys their age, the hockey players enjoy having a good time and living for the moment instead of living up to the town's expectations of them as heroes. They are however forced to grow up quickly as they face adult realities.

~~~

quiz question 8

Backman worked as a _____ before he published his first novel. He worked during evening and weekend shifts so he could write during daytime.

~~~

~~~

quiz question 9

True or False: Backman grew up loving ice hockey, but it was the one sport he could not play as a child. He was fragile as a boy and always ended up injured every time he played it. There are things he finds dark about the sport despite his fascination with the game.

~~~

~~~

quiz question 10

Backman views writing as a_____, not as a career choice. His father thinks his writing is probably something that he won't be doing for the rest of his life and Backman himself agrees.

~~~

~~~

quiz question 11

True or False: Backman started writing his first novel as blog entries. People around him found his account of the man called Ove very funny. It was taken from a real life incident which he later on developed upon the advice of his readers.

~~~

~~~

quiz question 12

True or False: Backman admits he is better at telling stories than dealing with language. He rewrote his second novel 50 times but his third novel was rewritten five times. He has no real formula for writing his stories.

~~~

Quiz Answers

1. A Man Called Ove
2. Peter
3. True
4. False
5. True
6. Amat
7. True
8. Forklift driver
9. True
10. Hobby
11. True
12. True

Ways to Continue Your Reading

EVERY month, our team runs through a wide selection of books to pick the best titles for readers and reading groups, and promotes these titles to our thousands of readers – sometimes with free downloads, sale dates, and additional brochures.

Want to register yourself or a book group? It's free and takes 1-click.

Register here.

On the Next Page...

Please write us your reviews! Any length would be fine but we'd appreciate hearing you more! We'd be SO grateful.

Till next time,

BookHabits

"Loving Books is Actually a Habit"

Made in United States
Orlando, FL
26 May 2022

18208168R00039